Soon To Be Mr. & Mrs.

Wedding Date:

Wedding Planner

WEDDING DATE & TIME:

VENUE ADDRESS:

BUDGET:

OFFICIANT:

WEDDING PARTY:

TO DO LIST:

NOTES & REMINDERS:

Wedding Budget Planner

	TOTAL COST:	DEPOSIT:	REMAINDER:
WEDDING VENUE			
RECEPTION VENUE			
FLORIST			
OFFICIANT			
CATERER			
WEDDING CAKE			
BRIDAL ATTIRE			
GROOM ATTIRE			
BRIDAL JEWELRY			
BRIDESMAID ATTIRE			
GROOMSMEN ATTIRE			
HAIR & MAKE UP			
PHOTOGRAPHER			
VIDEOGRAPHER			
DJ SERVICE/ENTERTAINMENT			
INVITATIONS			
TRANSPORTATION			
WEDDING PARTY GIFTS			
RENTALS			
HONEYMOON			

12 Months Before

- [ ] SET THE DATE
- [ ] SET YOUR BUDGET
- [ ] CHOOSE YOUR THEME
- [ ] ORGANIZE ENGAGEMENT PARTY
- [ ] RESEARCH VENUES
- [ ] BOOK A WEDDING PLANNER
- [ ] RESEARCH PHOTOGRAPHERS
- [ ] RESEARCH VIDEOGRAPHERS
- [ ] RESEARCH DJ'S/ENTERTAINMENT

- [ ] CONSIDER FLORISTS
- [ ] RESEARCH CATERERS
- [ ] DECIDE ON OFFICIANT
- [ ] CREATE INITIAL GUEST LIST
- [ ] CHOOSE WEDDING PARTY
- [ ] SHOP FOR WEDDING DRESS
- [ ] REGISTER WITH GIFT REGISTRY
- [ ] DISCUSS HONEYMOON IDEAS
- [ ] RESEARCH WEDDING RINGS

THINGS TO REMEMBER:

9 Months Before

- FINALIZE GUEST LIST
- ORDER INVITATIONS
- PLAN YOUR RECEPTION
- BOOK PHOTOGRAPHER
- BOOK VIDEOGRAPHER
- BOOK FLORIST
- BOOK DJ/ENTERTAINMENT
- BOOK CATERER
- CHOOSE WEDDING CAKE

- CHOOSE WEDDING GOWN
- ORDER BRIDESMAIDS DRESSES
- RESERVE TUXEDOS
- ARRANGE TRANSPORTATION
- BOOK WEDDING VENUE
- BOOK RECEPTION VENUE
- PLAN HONEYMOON
- BOOK OFFICIANT
- BOOK ROOMS FOR GUESTS

THINGS TO REMEMBER:

6 Months Before

- [ ] ORDER THANK YOU NOTES
- [ ] REVIEW RECEPTION DETAILS
- [ ] MAKE APPT FOR DRESS FITTING
- [ ] CONFIRM BRIDEMAIDS DRESSES
- [ ] GET MARRIAGE LICENSE

- [ ] BOOK HAIR/MAKE UP STYLIST
- [ ] CONFIRM MUSIC SELECTIONS
- [ ] PLAN BRIDAL SHOWER
- [ ] PLAN REHEARSAL
- [ ] SHOP FOR WEDDING RINGS

THINGS TO REMEMBER:

3 Months Before

- [ ] MAIL OUT INVITATIONS
- [ ] MEET WITH OFFICIANT
- [ ] BUY GIFTS FOR WEDDING PARTY
- [ ] BOOK FINAL GOWN FITTING
- [ ] BUY WEDDING BANDS
- [ ] PLAN YOUR HAIR STYLE
- [ ] PURCHASE SHOES/HEELS
- [ ] CONFIRM PASSPORTS ARE VALID

- [ ] FINALIZE RECEPTION MENU
- [ ] PLAN REHEARSAL DINNER
- [ ] CONFIRM ALL BOOKINGS
- [ ] APPLY FOR MARRIAGE LICENSE
- [ ] CONFIRM MUSIC SELECTIONS
- [ ] DRAFT WEDDING VOWS
- [ ] CHOOSE YOUR MC
- [ ] ARRANGE AIRPORT TRANSFER

THINGS TO REMEMBER:

1 Month Before

- [ ] CONFIRM FINAL GUEST COUNT
- [ ] CONFIRM RECEPTION DETAILS
- [ ] ATTEND FINAL GOWN FITTING
- [ ] CONFIRM PHOTOGRAPHER
- [ ] WRAP WEDDING PARTY GIFTS
- [ ] CREATE PHOTOGRAPHY SHOT LIST

- [ ] REHEARSE WEDDING VOWS
- [ ] BOOK MANI-PEDI
- [ ] CONFIRM WITH FLORIST
- [ ] CONFIRM VIDEOGRAPHER
- [ ] PICK UP BRIDEMAIDS DRESSES
- [ ] CREATE WEDDING SCHEDULE

THINGS TO REMEMBER:

1 Week Before

- [ ] FINALIZE SEATING PLANS
- [ ] MAKE PAYMENTS TO VENDORS
- [ ] PACK FOR HONEYMOON
- [ ] CONFIRM HOTEL RESERVATIONS
- [ ] GIVE SCHEDULE TO PARTY

- [ ] DELIVER LICENSE TO OFFICIANT
- [ ] CONFIRM WITH BAKERY
- [ ] PICK UP WEDDING DRESS
- [ ] PICK UP TUXEDOS
- [ ] GIVE MUSIC LIST TO DJ

THINGS TO REMEMBER:

1 Day Before

- [ ] GET MANICURE/PEDICURE
- [ ] ATTEND REHEARSAL DINNER
- [ ] GET A GOOD NIGHT'S SLEEP!
- [ ] GIVE GIFTS TO WEDDING PARTY
- [ ] FINALIZE PACKING

TO DO LIST:

The Big Day!

- [ ] GET HAIR & MAKE UP DONE
- [ ] HAVE A HEALTHY BREAKFAST
- [ ] ENJOY YOUR BIG DAY!

- [ ] MEET WITH BRIDESMAIDS
- [ ] GIVE RINGS TO BEST MAN

TO DO LIST:

Wedding Planner

ENGAGEMENT PARTY:

DATE: _____

LOCATION: _____

TIME: _____

NUMBER OF GUESTS: _____

NOTES:

BRIDAL SHOWER:

DATE: _____

LOCATION: _____

TIME: _____

NUMBER OF GUESTS: _____

NOTES:

STAG & DOE PARTY:

DATE: _____

LOCATION: _____

TIME: _____

NUMBER OF GUESTS: _____

NOTES:

Wedding Party

MAID/MATRON OF HONOR:

PHONE: _____ DRESS SIZE: _____ SHOE SIZE: _____

EMAIL: _____

BRIDESMAID:

PHONE: _____ DRESS SIZE: _____ SHOE SIZE: _____

EMAIL: _____

BRIDESMAID #2:

PHONE: _____ DRESS SIZE: _____ SHOE SIZE: _____

EMAIL: _____

BRIDESMAID #3:

PHONE: _____ DRESS SIZE: _____ SHOE SIZE: _____

EMAIL: _____

BRIDESMAID #4:

PHONE: _____ DRESS SIZE: _____ SHOE SIZE: _____

EMAIL: _____

NOTES:

Wedding Party

BEST MAN:

PHONE: _____ WAIST SIZE: _____ SHOE SIZE: _____

NECK SIZE: _____ SLEEVE SIZE: _____ JACKET SIZE: _____

EMAIL: _____

GROOMSMEN #1:

PHONE: _____ WAIST SIZE: _____ SHOE SIZE: _____

NECK SIZE: _____ SLEEVE SIZE: _____ JACKET SIZE: _____

EMAIL: _____

GROOMSMEN #2:

PHONE: _____ WAIST SIZE: _____ SHOE SIZE: _____

NECK SIZE: _____ SLEEVE SIZE: _____ JACKET SIZE: _____

EMAIL: _____

GROOMSMEN #3:

PHONE: _____ WAIST SIZE: _____ SHOE SIZE: _____

NECK SIZE: _____ SLEEVE SIZE: _____ JACKET SIZE: _____

EMAIL: _____

GROOMSMEN #4:

PHONE: _____ WAIST SIZE: _____ SHOE SIZE: _____

NECK SIZE: _____ SLEEVE SIZE: _____ JACKET SIZE: _____

EMAIL: _____

Photographer

PHOTOGRAPHER:

PHONE: _____   COMPANY: _____

EMAIL: _____   ADDRESS: _____

_____

WEDDING PACKAGE OVERVIEW:

EST PRICE: _____

INCLUSIONS:	YES ✓	NO ✓	COST:
ENGAGEMENT SHOOT:	☐	☐	_____
PHOTO ALBUMS:	☐	☐	_____
FRAMES:	☐	☐	_____
PROOFS INCLUDED:	☐	☐	_____
NEGATIVES INCLUDED:	☐	☐	_____

TOTAL COST: _____

Videographer

VIDEOGRAPHER:

PHONE: _____   COMPANY: _____

EMAIL: _____   ADDRESS: _____

_____

WEDDING PACKAGE OVERVIEW:

EST PRICE: _____

INCLUSIONS:	YES ✓	NO ✓	COST:
DUPLICATES/COPIES:	☐	☐	_____
PHOTO MONTAGE:	☐	☐	_____
MUSIC ADDED:	☐	☐	_____
EDITING:	☐	☐	_____

TOTAL COST: _____

NOTES:

DJ/Entertainment

DJ/LIVE BAND/ENTERTAINMENT:

PHONE: _____   COMPANY: _____

EMAIL: _____   ADDRESS: _____

START TIME: _____   END TIME: _____

ENTERTAINMENT SERVICE OVERVIEW:

EST PRICE: _____

INCLUSIONS:	YES ✓	NO ✓	COST:
SOUND EQUIPMENT:	☐	☐	_____
LIGHTING:	☐	☐	_____
SPECIAL EFFECTS:	☐	☐	_____
GRATUITIES	☐	☐	_____

TOTAL COST: _____

NOTES:

Florist

FLORIST:

PHONE: _____   COMPANY: _____

EMAIL: _____   ADDRESS: _____

FLORAL PACKAGE:

EST PRICE: _____

INCLUSIONS:	YES ✓	NO ✓	COST:
BRIDAL BOUQUET:	☐	☐	_____
THROW AWAY BOUQUET:	☐	☐	_____
CORSAGES:	☐	☐	_____
CEREMONY FLOWERS	☐	☐	_____
CENTERPIECES	☐	☐	_____
CAKE TOPPER	☐	☐	_____
BOUTONNIERE	☐	☐	_____

TOTAL COST: _____

Wedding Cake/Baker

PHONE: _____   COMPANY: _____

EMAIL: _____   ADDRESS: _____

WEDDING CAKE PACKAGE:

COST: _____   FREE TASTING: _____   DELIVERY FEE: _____

FLAVOR: _____

FILLING: _____

SIZE: _____

SHAPE: _____

COLOR: _____

EXTRAS: _____

TOTAL COST: _____

NOTES:

Transportation Planner

TO CEREMONY: PICK UP TIME: PICK UP LOCATION:

BRIDE:

GROOM:

BRIDE'S PARENTS:

GROOM'S PARENTS:

BRIDESMAIDS:

GROOMSMEN:

NOTES:

TO RECEPTION: PICK UP TIME: PICK UP LOCATION:

BRIDE & GROOM:

BRIDE'S PARENTS:

GROOM'S PARENTS:

BRIDESMAIDS:

GROOMSMEN:

Wedding Planner

BACHELORETTE PARTY:

DATE: _____   LOCATION: _____

TIME: _____   NUMBER OF GUESTS: _____

NOTES:

BACHELOR PARTY:

DATE: _____   LOCATION: _____

TIME: _____   NUMBER OF GUESTS: _____

NOTES:

CEREMONY REHEARSAL:

DATE: _____   LOCATION: _____

TIME: _____   NUMBER OF GUESTS: _____

NOTES:

Wedding Planner

REHEARSAL DINNER:

DATE: _____

TIME: _____

LOCATION: _____

NUMBER OF GUESTS: _____

NOTES:

RECEPTION:

DATE: _____

TIME: _____

LOCATION: _____

NUMBER OF GUESTS: _____

NOTES:

REMINDERS:

_____

_____

_____

_____

Names & Addresses

CEREMONY:

PHONE: _____   CONTACT NAME: _____

EMAIL: _____   ADDRESS: _____

RECEPTION:

PHONE: _____   CONTACT NAME: _____

EMAIL: _____   ADDRESS: _____

OFFICIANT:

PHONE: _____   CONTACT NAME: _____

EMAIL: _____   ADDRESS: _____

WEDDING PLANNER:

PHONE: _____   CONTACT NAME: _____

EMAIL: _____   ADDRESS: _____

CATERER:

PHONE: _____   CONTACT NAME: _____

EMAIL: _____   ADDRESS: _____

FLORIST:

PHONE: _____   CONTACT NAME: _____

EMAIL: _____   ADDRESS: _____

Names & Addresses

BAKERY:

PHONE: _____

EMAIL: _____

CONTACT NAME: _____

ADDRESS: _____

BRIDAL SHOP:

PHONE: _____

EMAIL: _____

CONTACT NAME: _____

ADDRESS: _____

PHOTOGRAPHER:

PHONE: _____

EMAIL: _____

CONTACT NAME: _____

ADDRESS: _____

VIDEOGRAPHER:

PHONE: _____

EMAIL: _____

CONTACT NAME: _____

ADDRESS: _____

DJ/ENTERTAINMENT:

PHONE: _____

EMAIL: _____

CONTACT NAME: _____

ADDRESS: _____

HAIR/NAIL SALON:

PHONE: _____

EMAIL: _____

CONTACT NAME: _____

ADDRESS: _____

Names & Addresses

MAKE UP ARTIST:

PHONE: _____   CONTACT NAME: _____

EMAIL: _____   ADDRESS: _____

RENTALS:

PHONE: _____   CONTACT NAME: _____

EMAIL: _____   ADDRESS: _____

HONEYMOON RESORT/HOTEL:

PHONE: _____   CONTACT NAME: _____

EMAIL: _____   ADDRESS: _____

TRANSPORTATION SERVICE:

PHONE: _____   CONTACT NAME: _____

EMAIL: _____   ADDRESS: _____

NOTES:

Caterer Details

CONTACT INFORMATION:

PHONE: _____

CONTACT NAME: _____

EMAIL: _____

ADDRESS: _____

MENU CHOICE #1:

MENU CHOICE #2:

	YES ✓	NO ✓	COST:
BAR INCLUDED:	☐	☐	_____
CORKAGE FEE:	☐	☐	_____
HORS D'OEUVRES:	☐	☐	_____
TAXES INCLUDED:	☐	☐	_____
GRATUITIES INCLUDED:	☐	☐	_____

Menu Planner

HORS D'OEUVRES

1st COURSE:

2nd COURSE:

3rd COURSE:

4th COURSE:

DESSERT:

1 Week Before

	THINGS TO DO:	NOTES:
MONDAY		
TUESDAY		
WEDNESDAY		
THURSDAY		

REMINDERS & NOTES:

1 Week Before

	THINGS TO DO:	NOTES:
FRIDAY		
SATURDAY		
SUNDAY		

LEFT TO DO:

REMINDERS:

NOTES:

Wedding Guest List

NAME:	ADDRESS:	# IN PARTY:	RSVP: ✓

Wedding Guest List

NAME:	ADDRESS:	# IN PARTY:	RSVP: ✓

Wedding Guest List

NAME:	ADDRESS:	# IN PARTY:	RSVP: ✓

Wedding Guest List

NAME:	ADDRESS:	# IN PARTY:	RSVP: ✓

Wedding Guest List

NAME:	ADDRESS:	# IN PARTY:	RSVP: ✓

Wedding Guest List

NAME:	ADDRESS:	# IN PARTY:	RSVP: ✓

Wedding Guest List

NAME:	ADDRESS:	# IN PARTY:	RSVP: ✓

Wedding Guest List

NAME:	ADDRESS:	# IN PARTY:	RSVP: ✓

Wedding Guest List

NAME:	ADDRESS:	# IN PARTY:	RSVP: ✓

Wedding Guest List

NAME:	ADDRESS:	# IN PARTY:	RSVP: ✓

Wedding Guest List

NAME:	ADDRESS:	# IN PARTY:	RSVP: ✓

Wedding Guest List

NAME:	ADDRESS:	# IN PARTY:	RSVP: ✓

Wedding Guest List

NAME:	ADDRESS:	# IN PARTY:	RSVP: ✓

Wedding Guest List

NAME:	ADDRESS:	# IN PARTY:	RSVP: ✓

Wedding Guest List

NAME:	ADDRESS:	# IN PARTY:	RSVP: ✓

Wedding Guest List

NAME:	ADDRESS:	# IN PARTY:	RSVP: ✓

Wedding Guest List

NAME:	ADDRESS:	# IN PARTY:	RSVP: ✓

Wedding Guest List

NAME:	ADDRESS:	# IN PARTY:	RSVP: ✓

Wedding Guest List

NAME:	ADDRESS:	# IN PARTY:	RSVP: ✓

Wedding Guest List

NAME:	ADDRESS:	# IN PARTY:	RSVP: ✓

Wedding Guest List

NAME:	ADDRESS:	# IN PARTY:	RSVP: ✓

Wedding Guest List

NAME:	ADDRESS:	# IN PARTY:	RSVP: ✓

Wedding Guest List

NAME:	ADDRESS:	# IN PARTY:	RSVP: ✓

Wedding Guest List

NAME:	ADDRESS:	# IN PARTY:	RSVP: ✓

Wedding Guest List

NAME:	ADDRESS:	# IN PARTY:	RSVP: ✓

Wedding Guest List

NAME:	ADDRESS:	# IN PARTY:	RSVP: ✓

Wedding Guest List

NAME:	ADDRESS:	# IN PARTY:	RSVP: ✓

Wedding Guest List

NAME:	ADDRESS:	# IN PARTY:	RSVP: ✓

Wedding Guest List

NAME:	ADDRESS:	# IN PARTY:	RSVP: ✓

Wedding Guest List

NAME:	ADDRESS:	# IN PARTY:	RSVP: ✓

Wedding Guest List

NAME:	ADDRESS:	# IN PARTY:	RSVP: ✓

Wedding Guest List

NAME:	ADDRESS:	# IN PARTY:	RSVP: ✓

Wedding Guest List

NAME:	ADDRESS:	# IN PARTY:	RSVP: ✓

Wedding Guest List

NAME:	ADDRESS:	# IN PARTY:	RSVP: ✓

Wedding Guest List

NAME:	ADDRESS:	# IN PARTY:	RSVP: ✓

Wedding Guest List

NAME:	ADDRESS:	# IN PARTY:	RSVP: ✓

Wedding Guest List

NAME:	ADDRESS:	# IN PARTY:	RSVP: ✓

Wedding Guest List

NAME:	ADDRESS:	# IN PARTY:	RSVP: ✓

Wedding Guest List

NAME:	ADDRESS:	# IN PARTY:	RSVP: ✓

Wedding Guest List

NAME:	ADDRESS:	# IN PARTY:	RSVP: ✓

Wedding Guest List

NAME:	ADDRESS:	# IN PARTY:	RSVP: ✓

Wedding Guest List

NAME:	ADDRESS:	# IN PARTY:	RSVP: ✓

Wedding Guest List

NAME:	ADDRESS:	# IN PARTY:	RSVP: ✓

Wedding Guest List

NAME:	ADDRESS:	# IN PARTY:	RSVP: ✓

Wedding Guest List

NAME:	ADDRESS:	# IN PARTY:	RSVP: ✓

Wedding Guest List

NAME:	ADDRESS:	# IN PARTY:	RSVP: ✓

Wedding Guest List

NAME:	ADDRESS:	# IN PARTY:	RSVP: ✓

Wedding Guest List

NAME:	ADDRESS:	# IN PARTY:	RSVP: ✓

Wedding Guest List

NAME:	ADDRESS:	# IN PARTY:	RSVP: ✓

Wedding Guest List

NAME:	ADDRESS:	# IN PARTY:	RSVP: ✓

Wedding Guest List

NAME:	ADDRESS:	# IN PARTY:	RSVP: ✓

Wedding Guest List

NAME:	ADDRESS:	# IN PARTY:	RSVP: ✓

Wedding Guest List

NAME:	ADDRESS:	# IN PARTY:	RSVP: ✓

Wedding Guest List

NAME:	ADDRESS:	# IN PARTY:	RSVP: ✓

Wedding Guest List

NAME:	ADDRESS:	# IN PARTY:	RSVP: ✓

Wedding Guest List

NAME:	ADDRESS:	# IN PARTY:	RSVP: ✓

Wedding Guest List

NAME:	ADDRESS:	# IN PARTY:	RSVP: ✓

Wedding Guest List

NAME:	ADDRESS:	# IN PARTY:	RSVP: ✓

Wedding Guest List

NAME:	ADDRESS:	# IN PARTY:	RSVP: ✓

Wedding Guest List

NAME:	ADDRESS:	# IN PARTY:	RSVP: ✓

Wedding Guest List

NAME:	ADDRESS:	# IN PARTY:	RSVP: ✓

Wedding Guest List

NAME:	ADDRESS:	# IN PARTY:	RSVP: ✓

Seating Chart Planner

Table #

Table #

Table #

Table #

SEATING PLANNER NOTES:

Seating Chart Planner

Table #

Table #

Table #

Table #

SEATING PLANNER NOTES:

Seating Chart Planner

Table #

Table #

Table #

Table #

SEATING PLANNER NOTES:

Seating Chart Planner

Table #

Table #

Table #

Table #

SEATING PLANNER NOTES:

Seating Chart Planner

Table #

Table #

Table #

Table #

SEATING PLANNER NOTES:

Seating Chart Planner

Table #

Table #

Table #

Table #

SEATING PLANNER NOTES:

Seating Chart Planner

Table #

Table #

Table #

Table #

SEATING PLANNER NOTES:

Seating Chart Planner

Table #

Table #

Table #

Table #

SEATING PLANNER NOTES:

Seating Chart Planner

Table #

Table #

Table #

Table #

SEATING PLANNER NOTES:

Seating Chart Planner

Table #

Table #

Table #

Table #

SEATING PLANNER NOTES:

Seating Chart Planner

Table #

Table #

Table #

Table #

SEATING PLANNER NOTES:

Seating Chart Planner

Table #

Table #

Table #

Table #

SEATING PLANNER NOTES:

Seating Chart Planner

Table #

Table #

Table #

Table #

SEATING PLANNER NOTES:

Seating Chart Planner

Table #

Table #

Table #

Table #

SEATING PLANNER NOTES:

Seating Chart Planner

Table #

Table #

Table #

Table #

SEATING PLANNER NOTES:

Seating Chart Planner

Table #

Table #

Table #

Table #

SEATING PLANNER NOTES:

Seating Chart Planner

Table #

Table #

Table #

Table #

SEATING PLANNER NOTES:

Seating Chart Planner

Table #

Table #

Table #

Table #

SEATING PLANNER NOTES:

Seating Chart Planner

Table #

Table #

Table #

Table #

SEATING PLANNER NOTES:

Seating Chart Planner

Table #

Table #

Table #

Table #

SEATING PLANNER NOTES:

Seating Chart Planner

Table #

Table #

Table #

Table #

SEATING PLANNER NOTES:

Seating Chart Planner

Table #

Table #

Table #

Table #

SEATING PLANNER NOTES:

Seating Chart Planner

Table #

Table #

Table #

Table #

SEATING PLANNER NOTES:

Seating Chart Planner

Table #

Table #

Table #

Table #

SEATING PLANNER NOTES:

Seating Chart Planner

Table #

Table #

Table #

Table #

SEATING PLANNER NOTES:

Seating Chart Planner

Table #

Table #

Table #

Table #

SEATING PLANNER NOTES:

Seating Chart Planner

Table #

Table #

Table #

Table #

SEATING PLANNER NOTES:

Seating Chart Planner

Table #

Table #

Table #

Table #

SEATING PLANNER NOTES:

Seating Chart Planner

Table #

Table #

Table #

Table #

SEATING PLANNER NOTES:

Seating Chart Planner

Table #

Table #

Table #

Table #

SEATING PLANNER NOTES:

Seating Chart Planner

Table #

Table #

Table #

Table #

SEATING PLANNER NOTES:

Seating Chart Planner

Table #

Table #

Table #

Table #

SEATING PLANNER NOTES:

Seating Chart Planner

Table #

Table #

Table #

Table #

SEATING PLANNER NOTES:

Seating Chart Planner

Table #

Table #

Table #

Table #

SEATING PLANNER NOTES:

Seating Chart Planner

Table #

Table #

Table #

Table #

SEATING PLANNER NOTES:

Seating Chart Planner

Table #

Table #

Table #

Table #

SEATING PLANNER NOTES:

Seating Chart Planner

Table #

Table #

Table #

Table #

SEATING PLANNER NOTES:

Seating Chart Planner

Table #

Table #

Table #

Table #

SEATING PLANNER NOTES:

Seating Chart Planner

Table #

Table #

Table #

Table #

SEATING PLANNER NOTES:

Seating Chart Planner

Table #

Table #

Table #

Table #

SEATING PLANNER NOTES:

Seating Chart Planner

Table #

Table #

Table #

Table #

SEATING PLANNER NOTES:

Seating Chart Planner

Table #

Table #

Table #

Table #

SEATING PLANNER NOTES:

Seating Chart Planner

Table #

Table #

Table #

Table #

SEATING PLANNER NOTES:

Seating Chart Planner

Table #

Table #

Table #

Table #

SEATING PLANNER NOTES:

Seating Chart Planner

Table #

Table #

Table #

Table #

SEATING PLANNER NOTES:

Seating Chart Planner

Table #

Table #

Table #

Table #

SEATING PLANNER NOTES:

Seating Chart Planner

Table #

Table #

Table #

Table #

SEATING PLANNER NOTES:

Seating Chart Planner

Table #

Table #

Table #

Table #

SEATING PLANNER NOTES:

Seating Chart Planner

Table #

Table #

Table #

Table #

SEATING PLANNER NOTES:

Seating Chart Planner

Table #

Table #

Table #

Table #

SEATING PLANNER NOTES:

Seating Chart Planner

Table #

Table #

Table #

Table #

SEATING PLANNER NOTES:

Seating Chart Planner

Table #

Table #

Table #

Table #

SEATING PLANNER NOTES:

Seating Chart Planner

Table #

Table #

Table #

Table #

SEATING PLANNER NOTES:

Seating Chart Planner

Table #

Table #

Table #

Table #

SEATING PLANNER NOTES:

Seating Chart Planner

Table #

Table #

Table #

Table #

SEATING PLANNER NOTES:

Seating Chart Planner

Table #

Table #

Table #

Table #

SEATING PLANNER NOTES:

Seating Chart Planner

Table #

Table #

Table #

Table #

SEATING PLANNER NOTES:

Seating Chart Planner

Table #

Table #

Table #

Table #

SEATING PLANNER NOTES:

Made in the USA
Middletown, DE
09 May 2022

65528456R00090